TAMING THE HUSKIES

UNDERDOGS

SPORTS CHAMPIONS

★
★
★

★

★

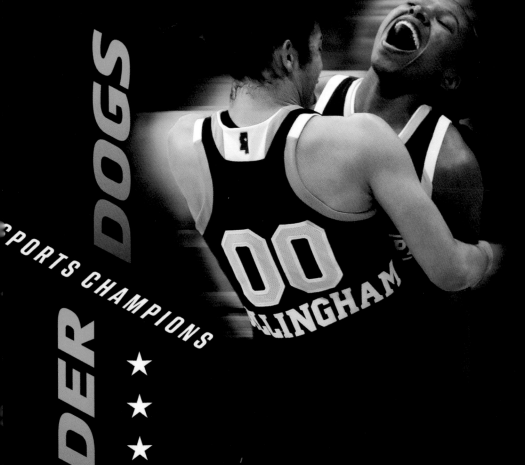

BY MARTIN GITLIN

45TH PARALLEL PRESS

Published in the United States of America by Cherry Lake Publishing Group
Ann Arbor, Michigan
www.cherrylakepublishing.com

Reading Adviser: Beth Walker Gambro, MS, Ed., Reading Consultant, Yorkville, IL
Series Adviser: Virginia Loh-Hagan
Book Designer: Jen Wahi

Photo Credits: cover: © Aaron M. Sprecher via AP; page 5: © Alayna Stevens/The Reflector; page 7: © Alayna Stevens/
The Reflector; page 9: © Aaron M. Sprecher via AP; page 13: © Cal Sport Media via AP Images; page 15: © Alayna Stevens/
The Reflector; page 17: © AP Photo/Tony Gutierrez; page 21: © Alayna Stevens/The Reflector; page 25: © AP Photo/Tony
Gutierrez; page 29: © AP Photo/Eric Gay

45th Parallel Press is an imprint of Cherry Lake Publishing Group.

Library of Congress Cataloging-in-Publication Data

Names: Gitlin, Martin, author.
Title: Taming the Huskies / written by Martin Gitlin.
Description: Ann Arbor, Michigan : 45th Parallel Press, 2023. | Series:
   Underdogs. Sports champions | Audience: Grades 4-6 | Summary: "Taming
   the Huskies takes readers inside the famous 2017 women's NCAA basketball
   game between the Connecticut Huskies and the Mississippi State Bulldogs.
   Provides background leading up to the game, review of the game, why the
   world was shocked, and what happened afterward. From players no one
   believed in to teams no one thought could win, Underdogs: Sports
   Champions covers some of history's greatest underdogs. Written in a
   strong narrative nonfiction style, the storytelling in these books will
   captivate readers. The series includes considerate vocabulary, engaging
   content, clear text and formatting, and compelling photos. Educational
   sidebars include extra fun facts and information"-- Provided by
   publisher.
Identifiers: LCCN 2023005884 | ISBN 9781668927779 (hardcover) | ISBN
   9781668928820 (paperback) | ISBN 9781668930298 (ebook) | ISBN
   9781668931776 (pdf)
Subjects: LCSH: Mississippi State Bulldogs (Basketball team)--Juvenile
   literature. | Connecticut Huskies (Basketball team)--Juvenile
   literature. | NCAA Women's Basketball Tournament (2017 : Dallas, Tex.)
Classification: LCC GV885.43.M57 G57 2023 | DDC
   796.323/6309762953--dc23/eng/20230222
LC record available at https://lccn.loc.gov/2023005884

Cherry Lake Publishing would like to acknowledge the work of the Partnership for 21st Century Learning, a network of
Battelle for Kids. Please visit http://www.battelleforkids.org/networks/p21 for more information.

Note from publisher: Websites change regularly, and their future contents are outside of our control. Supervise children when
conducting any recommended online searches for extended learning opportunities.

Printed in the United States of America
Corporate Graphics

TABLE OF CONTENTS

Introduction

What makes sports fun? Fans love watching sports. They love watching great athletes. They love seeing the best in action. They're awed by their skills. They're awed by their talent.

But what makes sports interesting? One never knows what will happen. Fans can expect an outcome. Their side could win. Or their side could lose. Nobody knows for sure.

Sometimes an upset happens. This is when a team that's expected to win loses. Upsets make fans sad. They confuse people.

Sometimes an underdog rises to the top. Underdogs can be players. They can be teams. They have little chance of winning. Yet, they win.

Morgan William controls the ball in the Mississippi State Bulldogs' game against the University of Connecticut Huskies.

5

Surprises happen. They're shocking. But they're wonderful. They're fun to watch.

That's why games are played. That's why fans watch games. They don't know who's going to win. They don't know who's going to lose. This is the point of sports. Not knowing is exciting.

Upsets in sports are legends. Legends are great stories. They're remembered forever. Underdogs make people smile. They inspire. They give hope. There are many sports champions. The most loved are underdogs. This series is about them.

Teaira McCowan and Blair Schaefer join in a huddle with Coach Vic Schaefer before the start of their game against the UConn Huskies.

Warming Up

Women's college sports changed in the 1970s and 1980s. Laws changed. They promoted equality. Female athletes had more opportunities. They started to play the same events as men.

One event was March Madness. This is a basketball tournament. Tournaments are a series of contests. They decide a champion. This tournament takes place in March.

Men have played in March Madness since 1939. Women weren't allowed. They weren't given the chance. College sports had been a man's world. But not in 1982. That's when the women's event began.

One problem remained in 2017. There was little depth in the women's game. Not enough schools had good players.

Ketara Chapel, forward for the Mississippi State Bulldogs, gets ready for a pass during the NCAA Final Four game against the UConn Huskies. No one expected the Bulldogs to win.

Most went to the same schools. They wanted to play with the best basketball programs.

That had bad results. The same 2 teams won year after year. One was the University of Tennessee. The other was the University of Connecticut.

Those 2 schools dominated. The University of Tennessee Volunteers had earned 8 titles. They've done this since 1987. The University of Connecticut Huskies had won 11 titles. They had only lost once in 3 years.

That was great for the Huskies. But it wasn't great for the sport. Other teams needed to step up. Someone had to beat these teams. Few expected that to happen in 2017. The Huskies were still on top.

The Huskies were ahead in the 2017 finals. They were leading 36–0. But that doesn't tell the whole story. The Huskies had battered foes all year. They beat San Francisco. The score was 102–37. They beat East Carolina. The score was 91–44. They beat Tulsa. The score was 105–57. Big wins were supposed to end with March Madness. But they didn't. The Huskies buried Albany. The score was 116–55. They beat Syracuse. The score was 94–64. They beat Oregon. The score was 90–52. No team could keep up with the Huskies. They had a great offense. Offense is playing to score. The Huskies scored 87 points per game that year. Two players averaged more than 20 points per game. They were Napheesa Collier and Katie Lou Samuelson. They were super long-distance shooters. Both made more than 40 percent of their 3-pointers. These are shots from beyond the 3-point line. Shots made from closer are worth only 2 points.

The Upset

The Mississippi State Bulldogs had a fine team in 2017. They won their first 21 games. Few thought they could beat the Huskies. But they were playing great.

Winning early in the season doesn't matter. Playing your best heading into March Madness matters. Teams want to peak for the tournament. And the Bulldogs didn't. They began to lose. They lost twice to South Carolina. They lost to Kentucky. They lost to Tennessee. They were only ranked number 7.

The Huskies were number 1 for years. They knew all about the Bulldogs. They knocked the Bulldogs out a year earlier. The Huskies didn't just beat them in 2016. They clobbered them. Their final score was 98–38.

There was no reason to believe the Huskies would fail. They were on top in 2017. They had easily taken their first 4

Azura Williams (23) of the UConn Huskies gets control of a rebound in a 2017 game against Oklahoma. The Huskies were the best in the league. They'd had a great season.

tournament games. They had won them by an average of 35 points.

Meanwhile, the Bulldogs were struggling to win. They only beat Washington by 9 points. They needed overtime to take down Baylor. Overtime is an extra period. It's after regular playing time. It happens when there's a tied game.

The Huskies had more experience. They knew how to deal with pressure. They had played for titles year after year. Geno Auriemma was their coach. He was considered the best in basketball. His Huskies had battered the Bulldogs a year earlier. Most assumed it would happen again.

Vic Schaefer was the Bulldogs' coach. He felt his team was better than in 2016. He said, "I think we've grown from that day. And we've learned from it. We're going to do our very best to play a really good ballgame."

A really good ball game might not be enough. The Bulldogs needed to play better than their best. The Huskies would be a hard team to beat.

Dominique Dillingham plays a strong defense to stop UConn's Kia Nurse from making it down the court.

The Shocker

It was March 31. It was 2017. The Bulldogs were about to play the Huskies. The winner would advance to the NCAA title game.

Fans were all asking the same questions: Could the Bulldogs hang with the Huskies? Would the Huskies lead with a big point gap from the start? The Bulldogs would lose if that happened.

The opposite happened. The Bulldogs sprinted out to a lead. They scored 14 straight points. They forged ahead. They scored 29–13. It was one of the biggest losses the Huskies had faced in 22 years. The Huskies fought back. They took a 40–39 lead early. They did this in the second half. The teams fought back and forth from there.

Bulldog Dominique Dillingham (00) blocks UConn player Crystal Dangerfield (5) from shooting a basket.

The game was tied at 60–60. The Bulldogs had a chance to win. Morgan William played for the Bulldogs. She was a **guard**. A guard passes the ball. William shot the ball. Her shot was blocked. The buzzer sounded. The game remained tied.

The battle went into overtime. Both teams had a great defense. The score was 64–64. William had another chance to play hero. She dribbled the ball forward. Then she shot it. The ball fell through the hoop. It was over. The Bulldogs won. They had scored an upset.

The Huskies were stunned. They had a winning streak. They had won 111 games. Their streak was over.

William was thrilled. She said, "I live for moments like this. [The Huskies are] an incredible team. For me to make that shot against them, it's unbelievable. I'm still in shock right now . . . I wanted to take the shot and I made it." She had indeed made the shot. Her shot shocked the basketball world.

★ Morgan William is short. She's 5-foot-5. Her nickname is "Itty Bitty." She said, "It's cool. I mean everybody knows that . . . They say how Itty Bitty can get buckets."

★ William is from Ironside, Alabama. Her mother is a hairdresser. Her stepfather is an accountant. He taught her how to play basketball.

★ William is close to her stepfather. She has a tattoo. The tattoo is on her left side. It's of her stepfather's favorite Bible verse. It reads, "I can do all things through Christ who strengthens me."

★ William prays before every game.

★ William cleans the house when she's bored. She likes to have things in perfect order.

★ William's favorite food is chicken tenders. Her favorite dessert is brownies.

The Response

When Morgan William made the shot, she became a hero.
The Bulldogs went crazy. Players rushed onto the court.
They hugged William. They jumped up and down.
They hugged each other. They fell to the floor together.
The crowd screamed.

Coach Vic Schaefer picked William up. He hugged her
tightly. William was the smallest player on the court. But she
had made the biggest shot.

Schaefer was joyful. He knew his team had just made
history. He understood the greatness of Connecticut. That is
what made the moment so special. Schaefer said, "That is
one heck of a basketball team, the greatest of all time. But
how proud am I of my kids?"

Morgan William takes her game-winning shot during overtime in the Bulldogs' NCAA Final Four game against the UConn Huskies.

Coach Geno Auriemma was also proud of his players. He took the defeat well. He knew they had to lose at some time. He said, "I knew this was coming at some point. I'm just shocked that it took this long to get here . . . Nobody's won more than we've won. I understand losing." He understood it better on that night. His team had lost for the first time in nearly 3 years.

SAME SPORT, DIFFERENT STORY

Top college basketball teams ease into their seasons. They often play small schools. Small schools tend to be weaker. Such games give small schools big money. They earn this money from ticket sales. All schools gain more practice. The outcome is usually a big win for the big school. The University of Virginia Cavaliers was among those top schools in 1982. Its men's team had a superstar. His name was Ralph Sampson. He stood 7-foot-4. The Cavaliers were ranked No. 1. Their next game was to be an easy win. It was against tiny Chaminade. That school is in Hawaii. They were called the Silverswords. Few were paying attention. Fans assumed Virginia would clobber Chaminade. They assumed wrong. The Silverswords stayed close the whole game. Then they pulled away at the end. They won. The final score was 77–72. There have been many upsets in college basketball. But none bigger than that one.

★ ★

Moving On

The Bulldogs still had a job to do. They had stunned the Huskies. Fans were talking about it. But two nights later, they had to play again. This was an even bigger game. It was for the college basketball championship. The Bulldogs had never won one.

It'd be a tough task for the Bulldogs. Their opponent was the South Carolina Gamecocks. The Gamecocks had already beaten them twice that season. The Bulldogs wanted revenge. Revenge means getting even.

The Bulldogs wanted to beat the Gamecocks. They were ready to roll. They took an early lead. But the Gamecocks bounced back. Soon the Bulldogs fell far behind.

They recovered in the third quarter. Morgan William got on a roll. She stole the ball. She scored. Soon the Bulldogs

Bulldogs Jazzmun Holmes (10) and Teaira McCowan (15) guard the basket against South Carolina Gamecocks player A'ja Wilson (22) in the 2017 NCAA Finals.

were ahead. They were leading 48–44. But the Gamecocks gained the lead. The Bulldogs fell in the fourth quarter. They finally lost. The final score was 67–55. The Bulldogs had not made enough shots. They shot poorly. They tried to get 3-point shots. They tried 15 times. They didn't make any.

Vic Schaefer talked about the defeat. He had played the Gamecocks 9 times since becoming coach. And his teams had lost each one. He said, "Today doesn't define us. We had one heck of a year. Obviously, we've had some hard times dealing with them. Today was no different."

The Bulldogs did have a heck of a year. They did in 2018 as well. They reached the finals again before falling to

★

★

Women's basketball began being played in 1892. It started at Smith College. Smith College is in Massachusetts. Basketball became the first women's team sport. Senda Berenson Abbott worked at Smith College. She taught basketball. She wrote the first basketball guide for women. She was taking risks. Women weren't thought to be strong. They were expected to work at home. People worried playing games would be too much for women. Abbott changed the rules for women. People worried about what women would wear. Women wore pants for the first time. Men weren't allowed to watch. Women's basketball spread. It became more popular. Teams usually formed within colleges. But colleges soon played other colleges. The first women's college game was in 1896. Stanford played the University of California, Berkeley. Women's basketball became an Olympic sport in 1976. The first professional basketball league for women was formed in 1978.

Notre Dame. They had become a basketball power. The taming of the Huskies had started it all.

The upset of the Huskies changed everything. Women's college basketball was never the same. There were no longer 1 or 2 teams winning every year. Four different teams took the title from 1998 to 2002. Among them were Notre Dame and Stanford. Neither had won the title in nearly 20 years. The Huskies remained a top team. They reached the semifinals every season from 2017 to 2021. But they lost 4 years in a row. Other schools became big winners. Among them were Oregon, Stanford, and Louisville. Times had changed. And that was a good thing for women's college basketball.

The Bulldogs running in for a group hug after their win against the UConn Huskies. These underdogs changed NCAA women's basketball.

Learn More

Books

Carothers, Thomas. *Geno Auriemma and the Connecticut Huskies*. North Mankato, MN: Sportszone, 2018.

Doeden, Matt. *Coming Up Clutch: The Greatest Upsets, Comebacks, and Finishes in Sports History*. Minneapolis, MN: Millbrook Press, 2018.

Frederic Evans, John. *Geno Auriemma (Championship Coaches)*. New York, NY: Enslow Publishing, 2019.

Wilner, Barry. *Biggest Upsets of All Time*. North Mankato, MN: Sportszone, 2015.

Explore These Online Sources with an Adult:

Britannica Kids: Basketball

Kiddle.com: Basketball facts for kids

Sports Illustrated Kids: Basketball

Glossary

3-pointer (THREE POYN-ter) A long-distance shot worth 3 points

guard (GAARD) A Player often responsible for passing the ball and scoring

legend (LEH-juhnd) An extremely famous story that is told many times

overtime (OH-vuhr-tyem) An extra period played to determine a winner when regular time ends in a tie

revenge (ri-VENJ) Getting even against a team against which one has lost

tournament (TUR-nuh-muhnt) Games played to determine an overall champion

underdog (UHN-der-dawg) A player or team that has little chance of winning but ends up winning

upset (UHP-set) When the team that is expected to win loses

Index

About the Author

Martin Gitlin is a sports book author based in Cleveland. He won more than 45 awards as a newspaper sportswriter from 1991 to 2002. Marty has had more than 200 books published since 2006. Most were written for students.